Virtual Reality for Public Speaking

Overcoming Fear and Anxiety

Table of Contents

Chapter 1. Introduction

Unleash the power within and say goodbye to sweaty palms and stammering speeches! Our special report on "Virtual Reality for Public Speaking: Overcoming Fear and Anxiety" dives into accessible and groundbreaking solutions that promise to turn your public speaking anxieties into engaging and confidence-driven performances. This engaging report is artfully packed with practical tips, backed by cutting-edge research and real-life success stories. Whether you're a seasoned speaker seeking to refine your craft, or a novice trembling at the thought of your first speech, this transformative guide is a game-changer. Discover true panache and charisma hidden within you, and turn every stage into your personal podium! Get your hands on this special report today, because your voice matters, and it's time the world listened!

Chapter 2. Introduction to Virtual Reality and Public Speaking

If you've ever experienced the heart-racing, sweat-inducing anxiety that comes with public speaking, you're not alone. The fear of public speaking, or glossophobia, is a common phobia — statistics indicate that up to 75% of people experience some degree of anxiety or nervousness related to public speaking. In other words, three out of every four individuals have stood where you stand, feeling the same tension, fear, and apprehension. Suffice it to say, you're in good company.

But just because this fear is widespread doesn't mean it's insurmountable. With the advent of technology and innovation, unique and effective methods to combat public speaking anxiety are emerging. One such potential solution, which this special report focuses on, is virtual reality.

2.1. Why Virtual Reality?

Virtual reality (VR) is often directly linked with gaming and entertainment. However, with extensive and evolving capabilities, it's increasingly used in a variety of other fields, like therapy, training, education, design, and importantly for this guide, public speaking.

So, what is Virtual Reality? VR is a simulated experience created with computer technology, which can be similar to or entirely different from the physical world. Devices such as VR headsets fully immerses users in the simulation, engaging multiple senses, including sight, hearing, and sometimes touch, to create as authentic an experience as possible.

This immersive technology can be leveraged to provide a safe and controlled virtual environment in which to practice public speaking skills. Within the VR simulation, any necessary scenario can be created, from a boardroom of challenging executives to a auditorium filled with thousands of attendees. It provides the opportunity to practice and experience public speaking in a variety of scenarios without any real-world consequences. Virtual reality can replicate the stress-inducing elements of public speaking, creating an opportunity to manage and mitigate anxiety in a risk-free, feedback-rich environment.

2.2. The Connection: Public Speaking and Virtual Reality

Given the potential effects of glossophobia on personal and professional success, finding working remedies for these anxieties can shape the trajectory of one's life. VR, owing to its imitable and highly customizable nature, has proven a promising tool in tackling this widespread fear.

The concept is backed by a theoretical framework known as 'exposure therapy'. Exposure therapy is a psychological treatment that helps people confront their fears. The fundamental idea is to create a safe environment that exposes the individual to the feared object or context without any danger, in order to overcome their anxiety.

In the realm of public speaking, VR serves as a precise tool to replicate the anxiety-inducing atmosphere while maintaining the safety of the simulated setting. People can confront their fear of speaking in front of an audience, learn to manage their anxiety, and build confidence.

Additional advantages of VR for public speaking extend beyond the imitation of challenging situations. It provides instant feedback on performance, from body language and volume control, right down to filler word usage. Over time, by gradually increasing the complexity and intensity of the VR scenarios, the individual can practice, improve skills, and build a healthier psychological response to the situation of speaking in public.

Virtual reality is a potent, immersive tool that brings flexibility, safety, and adaptability right to your living room. It has the capacity to replicate a breadth of scenarios, monitor performance, and accelerate the skill-building process. In short, it offers a dynamic solution to a universal fear.

2.3. Virtual Reality and Beyond

Stepping away from just the technical logistics, there's another way VR can be beneficial for public speaking training — breaking mental barriers. Scientific studies report that the human brain often struggles to differentiate simulated VR experiences from real ones. This blurred line is powerful, as it presents an opportunity to change our perception and create new, positive mental pathways.

Experiencing successful public speaking within VR aids in overcoming the mental barriers associated with the fear of public speaking. It builds cognitive confidence, changes the perception of public speaking from a fear-inducing task to a conquerable challenge. The same confidence, when extrapolated to the real world, paves the way to successful real-life public speaking experiences.

Confidence, skills adapting to different scenarios, learnings from instant feedback - the culmination of all these mold you into a better speaker, capable of handling and overcoming the anxiety related to public speaking.

Circling back to where we started, it's pertinent to note that fears and phobias are not ideal, but they are human. It's overcoming this fear, with the aid of new and powerful technology, that presents an opportunity for growth, for evolution, and for transformation.

As we journey deeper into this report, you'll discover the scientific research that backs the use of VR for public speaking, explore how to leverage VR, and hear empowering stories from real-life individuals who've used VR technology to overcome their speaking anxiety. Welcome to this voyage of transformation, where inhibitions are left behind and a world of confident communication awaits!

Chapter 3. Exploring Fear and Anxiety in Public Speaking

The first step in addressing fear and anxiety related to public speaking is to understand these reactions to their core. They are not signs of weakness or incompetence but natural responses of our bodies to potential threats, tangible or intangible. This primal 'flight or fight' instinct, coupled with societal pressures and personal insecurities, often translates into performance anxiety — an unwelcome guest during public presentations. Let's dive deeper to explore these nitty-gritty details.

3.1. The Science Behind Fear and Anxiety

The physical symptoms of public speaking anxiety — shortness of breath, sweaty palms, trembling knees — can be traced back to our primitive ancestors. Back in the day, humans faced numerous immediate and deadly threats. Relying on our evolved response system, our bodies flood with adrenaline when faced with perceived danger, leading to increased heart rate and sweaty palms – all designed to enhance our ability to either fight or flee.

The issues emerge when this system is activated during situations that aren't physically threatening, such as delivering a public speech. However, our bodies can't differentiate between facing a wild animal and an audience. Both situations trigger the same physiological response — the stimulation of the sympathetic nervous system releasing cortisol and adrenaline, increasing heart rate and blood pressure, inhibiting digestion, and elevating blood sugar levels. These changes reverberate through our bodies, manifesting in the typical symptoms of public speaking anxiety.

Understanding that your body is only trying to protect you can sometimes help accept and manage the physical symptoms of stage fright. Furthermore, holistic approaches involving practice, cognitive restructuring, and introducing your body to 'safe' stress can help create new, healthier response patterns.

3.2. Society's Role in Enhancing Public Speaking Anxiety

On top of our innate primal responses, societal pressures often magnify the anxiety surrounding public speaking. We live in a world that highly values effective and charismatic speakers. From standing out in classroom discussions, acing job interviews, to leading team meetings, verbal dexterity and self-confidence are greatly prized. Consequently, the fear of underperforming and the resulting social embarrassment amplify our dread and anxiety towards public speaking.

We not only worry about delivering the content correctly but obsess over perfect enunciation and pronunciation, compelling gestures, and engaging eye contact. The fear of forgetting lines, going blank, or stumbling over words adds another layer of apprehension.

This societal pressure to be a perfect speaker pushes many into the fear-of-failure trap. The perceived threat is not just immediate embarrassment but longer-term consequences such as damage to self-esteem, reputation, and in some cases, even career setbacks.

=== Inadequate Experience and Preparation

The fear of public speaking is most significant for novice speakers—people who have little to no experience in addressing an audience. This fear stems from their unfamiliarity with the process and environment of public speaking. It's common to feel anxious when undertaking an unfamiliar task. Lack of knowledge about writing speeches, creating engaging content, or modulating voice pitch contributes to the dread.

However, even seasoned speakers aren't immune to anxiety. Improper or inadequate preparation can induce stress. Rushing through the preparation phase, avoiding practice sessions, and relying solely on improvisation leads to a lack of control during the actual presentation, thereby inducing anxiety.

3.3. Journey of Self-Acceptance

Now that you understand the roots of your fear, you can approach it with a more mindful attitude. The fear or anxiety you feel is a part of many others' lives too, not a personal failing or shortcoming. You're not alone in this struggle; even successful public figures tend to get nervous before important speeches. Acknowledgment and acceptance are the first steps towards progress.

Embarking on this journey of managing and eventually overcoming your public speaking fear can elevate your personal and professional life. It's a journey of discovering and accepting yourself, learning to control your narrative, and expressing yourself with clarity and confidence.

The practice of noticing your unique anxiety symptoms can ground you in the present moment and help manage your anxiety better. Simple mindfulness practices such as focused breathing, visualization, and progressive muscle relaxation can deliver immediate relief.

3.4. Reconceptualizing 'Fear'

When you notice your 'fight or flight' response kicking in, try to reconceptualize it. Researchers have suggested that arousal or anxiety during public speaking can be beneficial if we can shift our perspective. Rather than seeing these physical symptoms as signs of fear, consider them evidence of your body preparing you to face a challenge or seize an opportunity.

=== Embrace Your Unique Speaking Style

Every speaker unique. Embrace your speaking style rather than yearning for the eloquence of successful public figures. Comparing yourself to others only increases anxiety and diminishes self-confidence. Strive for progress, not perfection.

With practice, patience, and self-compassion, you can start seeing your fear as part of a transformative journey towards becoming a confident, engaging speaker. Remember, Rome wasn't built in a day. With time and effort, you'll gradually see change, and before you know it, the stage will become your friend.

Chapter 4. Concluding Thoughts

The first step in overcoming the fear of public speaking is understanding and accepting it. Grasping the myriad reasons behind your anxiety can help build a rational, effective coping strategy. Remember, public speaking is a skill, not an inborn talent, and like any other skill, improvement comes with practice and experience.

Understanding that everyone has their unique style and pace reduces self-comparison and boosts confidence. With the advent of technology, specifically Virtual Reality, practicing presenting in different situations and environments is now possible in the comfort of your own home. This technology promises a future where public speaking isn't dreaded but embraced and enjoyed.

While the journey can seem daunting, the reward is immense. It is not just about conquering a fear or enhancing a skill; overcoming public speaking anxiety can be a transformative journey towards self-development, resilience, and self-expression. So it's about time we kick-start this journey. Because your voice matters, and the world needs to listen. In the upcoming chapters, we will dive into the specifics of how Virtual Reality can help you achieve this transformation. Until then, happy exploring!

Chapter 5. How Virtual Reality Technology Works

In order to better understand how virtual reality can assist in overcoming the fear of public speaking, it is essential to comprehend the technology behind it. Virtual Reality (VR) is a cutting-edge technology that can beguile the senses into experiencing a simulated environment as if it were the real one. This illusion is achieved by providing the user with artificial sensory feedback that corresponds to their interactions within the digital realm.

5.1. The Basics of Virtual Reality

Virtual Reality or VR, in its simplest definition, is a computer-generated simulation of a three-dimensional environment that can be interacted with, in a seemingly real or physical way, by a person using special electronic equipment.

At its core, VR technology involves three primary components: a computer/server to process and render the graphics, a high resolution, low latency headset - often bundled with headphones for sound - for immersive viewing and interaction, and sensors to track the user's motion within the environment.

5.2. The VR Headset: Gateway to the Virtual World

The VR headset is arguably the most crucial component of VR technology. It is the device worn on the user's head that displays the immersive, three-dimensional graphics, creating the illusion of existing in a virtual environment.

The headset has a number of sensors and gyroscopes that can track the user's head movement, translating these motions into correspondingly adjusted views in the simulated world. Most VR headsets are equipped with OLED or AMOLED screens for each eye that replicate a broad field of view, producing more lifelike images.

Moreover, the headset often contains integrated headphones to supplement the immersive visual experience with soundscape, creating an unmatched level of sensory immersion.

5.3. The Role of Controllers and Motion Sensors

While the headset is flooding the user's senses with realistic images and sounds, there are other equally significant pieces of equipment contributing to the entire immersive experience - the controllers and motion sensors.

Controllers are hand-held devices that allow the user to interact with the virtual environment, letting them touch, grab, or manipulate virtual objects. They are embedded with sensors that track their movements in 3D space, and translate them into actions within the virtual environment.

The motion sensors, often cameras or infrared sensors, are positioned in the user's environment to capture body movements and respond to where the user is standing or how they are moving. More advanced setups may include motion-tracking suits or gloves for more precise body and hand tracking, opening up possibilities for full-body simulations.

5.4. Creating Virtual Environments: The Role of Software

The software component of VR technology is responsible for creating the virtual environments and experiences. It requires high levels of graphical rendering to produce realistic scenarios.

Advanced software is designed to imitate real-world physics, incorporate high-resolution textures, and even replicate specific sounds associated with various interactions. For instance, it's not uncommon in VR simulations to hear the sounds of footsteps changing as the user switches between walking on a carpet, a tiled floor or a wooden bridge.

This creation of intricate virtual environments involves a legion of professionals, including graphic artists, programmers, sound engineers, and game designers, all working to make the environment as life-like as possible.

5.5. Combining All Components: The VR Experience

When the various components work seamlessly together - the VR headset, sensors, controllers, and the software - they create a VR experience that is so powerful it can trick the human brain into believing it's somewhere else. This is known as "presence", and it's the ultimate goal of any virtual reality technology - to make you feel "present" in an artificial world.

In conclusion, Virtual Reality technology is a perfect symphony of intricate hardware and software components, all working in sync to transport users into realistic virtual environments. The power of VR is its ability to simulate real-world experiences so authentically that the fear and anxiety triggered by these experiences can be encountered and managed in a safe, controlled environment - a feature that makes it an exciting and promising tool in overcoming public speaking anxiety.

With this understanding of how VR works as a foundation, we can now delve into how it can be specially tailored for public speaking training, and how it can help people overcome fear and anxiety associated with speaking publicly, transforming them into confident and effective communicators.

Chapter 6. Virtual Reality as a Training Ground

Virtual reality (VR) is an innovative and immersive technology that has been making waves across various industries, from gaming and entertainment to education and healthcare. One area gaining attention is the utilization of VR for public speaking training. In a simulated environment, training participants can practice their talk, engage with a virtual audience, and receive immediate feedback on their performance. All these without the nerve-wracking pressure of a real live audience.

6.1. Embracing the Virtual Arena

Virtual reality provides a safe, low-risk environment for practice. The benefit of using VR as a training ground for public speaking is the ability to curate a virtual environment that accurately mimics real-life scenarios. This involves creating audiences of different sizes, diversities, and responses. You can speak in a business meeting, a school lecture, or even a packed conference room, all in just one VR session.

One key element in public speaking is learning to cope with the array of audience responses. Here, VR shines by providing diverse and nuanced virtual audiences that simulate a myriad of reactions, from frequent interruptions, skeptical expressions, to enthusiastic applause. This range of audience reactions can be carefully controlled, allowing you to gradually increase your comfort level and better manage your anxiety.

6.2. Instant Feedback Loop – The Virtual Coach

Another valuable feature of VR training in public speaking is the virtual coach or instant feedback loop. This aspect tracks the caliber of your performance—monitoring everything from body language, voice modulation, pace, to eye contact. This data is immediately processed and interpreted to provide real-time feedback and suggestions for improvement. So, every time you rehearse your speech in virtual reality, not only do you experience speaking in front of an audience, but you also receive actionable recommendations to make your delivery better.

6.3. Heightening Speaker Engagement

The immersive nature of VR holds another trump card—enhancing speaker engagement. A well-known phenomenon in public speaking is the "imaginary audience," the notion that the speaker feels as if they're delivering their speech to a more critical audience than they truly are. This perceived pressure can exacerbate nervousness and apprehension in speakers.

Virtual reality helps combat this by creating a more real, interactive audience that you can visually and audibly engage with, thus reducing the tendency for your mind to fabricate intimidating scenarios. In return, this practice enhances your engagement levels and aids in forming organic connections with your future, real-life audience.

6.4. Iterative Learning and Experimentation

Beyond the utilities discussed so far, VR empowers you to experiment with various speaking styles, techniques, and mannerisms without the fear of "not getting it right the first time." It operates on an iterative model of learning – you practice, receive feedback, adjust, and try again, allowing for experimental, immersive, and experiential learning. You can venture to try humor, drama, storytelling, or even provocative statements - all these with the safety net that only a simulated environment can provide.

6.5. Case Studies: Success Stories in VR and Public Speaking

Several individuals and organizations have turned their public speaking fortunes with VR as their training ground. An exemplary case is Ovation, a public speaking VR software company, who claims that 20% of users reported a significant drop in public speaking anxiety after just one session.

Another inspiring story is of a TEDx event speaker who claimed her successful presentation was largely due to her multiple practice sessions in the VR environment. She was able to familiarize herself with the stage layout and lighting, rehearse her talk countless times to different virtual audiences, and manifest unshakeable confidence on the actual day.

6.6. Future Directions

As immersive technology continues to advance, we can expect related software to evolve accordingly. Future VR applications might incorporate advanced machine learning to offer personalised feedback, sophisticated audience behavior, and even emulate individualized stress triggers to equip speakers with the best possible preparation.

In conclusion, VR presents itself as a powerful training ground for public speakers. With its ability to mirror diverse real-life scenarios, provide real-time feedback, enhance engagement, allow iterative learning, the application of VR in overcoming fear and anxiety related to public speaking is nothing short of revolutionary. It's high time aspiring and accomplished speakers alike permit themselves to explore this high-tech tool that's tipped to redefine the public speaking landscape.

Chapter 7. Overcoming Fear with Virtual Reality Exposure

Understanding Fear and Anxiety in Public Speaking === Fear and anxiety result from the anticipation of a perceived threat. With regards to public speaking, the threat is often rooted in criticism, rejection, or failure. The evolutionary "fight-or-flight" response kicks in, culminating in a barrage of physical and psychological manifestations. Sweaty palms, a racing heart, a shaky voice, and an anxious mind are a few of the many symptoms faced by public speakers.

Medical and psychological research suggest that an effective way to manage, if not entirely eliminate, this fear and anxiety is by repeated exposure to the triggering situation. Called exposure therapy, this method has been harnessed by Virtual Reality (VR) technology, providing a groundbreaking solution to overcoming public speaking anxiety.

Understanding VR Exposure Therapy === Virtual Reality Exposure Therapy (VRET) is a form of cognitive-behavioral therapy that uses immersive VR technology to expose individuals to the situations or environments that cause them anxiety. This exposure occurs in a safe, controlled environment, allowing individuals to confront their fears without the risks associated with real-life scenarios.

The beauty of VRET lies in its ability to create realistic simulations, making the brain believe it's facing an actual scenario. With repeated exposure, the initial fear response diminishes, leading to habituation and eventual overcoming of that fear.

Applying VRET to Public Speaking === Applying VRET to public speaking involves creating a virtual environment mimicking various public speaking scenarios. These could range from a small boardroom meeting to a large conference keynote. Speech content, audience size, audience behavior, and environment can be customized to gradually increase the complexity and challenge the speaker's comfort zones.

VRET software typically provides real-time feedback, enabling speakers to analyze their performance and improve. The feedback mainly focuses on aspects like body language, voice modulation, pacing, and eye contact.

Practicing with VRET: A Step-by-Step Approach === 1. Choose the right Virtual Reality device: There are various VR devices available in the market, ranging from high-end setups to budget-friendly options. Select a device according to your comfort and budget.

1. Select a suitable Virtual Reality Exposure Program: Many VRET applications are tailored to public speaking. Most of them offer customizable scenarios and real-time feedback. Ensure that the chosen software is compatible with your VR device.

2. Begin with a simple, less intimidating scenario: If you're a novice speaker, start with a smaller virtual audience in a less formal setting. For seasoned speakers intending to refine their skills, choose a scenario that closely represents your most intimidating speaking scenario.

3. Use the real-time feedback: Pay attention to the feedback provided by the software. This is crucial for identifying areas of strength and improvement.

4. Gradually increase the complexity: As you become more comfortable, start increasing the complexity of the scenarios. Add more audience members, change the setting, or add difficult audience behaviors.

5. Practice frequently: The key to efficiency in VRET is regular practice. Try to undertake VR sessions at least a couple of times a week.

The Science Behind VRET Success Stories === Several studies have highlighted the success of VRET in lessening public speaking anxiety. In a study conducted by Anderson et al., 2013, participants who used VRET as part of their course significantly reduced their speech anxiety compared to their peers.

In addition, according to the survey by Pertaub, Slater, and Barker, 2002, individuals who trained with difficult audience behavior in VRET reported feeling more confident in real-life public speaking situations.

These studies emulate the fact that VRET, with its safe, controlled, and customized environment, is a powerful tool for overcoming public speaking fears. If utilized effectively, it holds the potential to unleash the exceptional speaker within you.

A Final Note === Transforming fear into confidence is not an overnight journey, it requires patience, perseverance, and practice. By leveraging the power of VR, you can learn to manage your anxieties, stage fears, and inhibitions. Remember, your voice holds power and deserves to be heard. With the help of VRET, not only can you conquer your fears, but also discover the confident, charismatic speaker within you! So embark on this transformative journey today, step into the virtual world and take command of the real one. Because your voice matters, and it's time the world listened!

Chapter 8. Practical VR Techniques for Anxiety Reduction

Virtual reality (VR) is a rapidly growing technology that allows users to experience and interact with a three-dimensional, computer-generated environment. VR has the potential to revolutionize many fields, including public speaking, by providing a safe and controlled space to practice and overcome anxieties.

8.1. Understanding the Basics of VR

The concept of VR might appear daunting, especially for non-tech individuals. However, it's necessary to comprehend the premise before we try to explore its practical utilities. It involves donning a VR headset, which allows the wearer to interact with a simulated environment. This simulated space can range from a quiet beach to a fully packed auditorium, designed to mimic the pressure of a live audience.

8.2. Identifying Your Fears through VR

One of the most potent uses of VR in anxiety reduction is identifying your specific fears. Often, people are not aware of their root fears, identifying public speaking generally as intimidating. However, it could be making eye contact, large crowds, forgotten lines, or any number of factors. Thankfully, VR technology can simulate different circumstances and aid in pinpointing your fears.

For instance, you could be placed in a setting where you are supposed to make eye contact with each member of the audience. As you attempt the exercise, you may realize that you struggle with maintaining prolonged eye contact. This exercise helps you to recognize your weak areas and work on them.

8.3. Leveraging VR for Exposure Therapy

Exposure therapy is a common technique for anxiety reduction, which involves facing and controlling fear in a controlled environment. VR aligns perfectly with this method, offering an environment that is both safe and adjustable.

As a effective practice, start with less intimidating scenarios. These might involve presenting to a few virtual individuals or reciting a prepared speech. As your comfort level increases, you can adjust the parameters to make the experience more daunting — a larger audience, an unprepared speech, or a more formal setting. This technique helps you to build your comfort level step by step.

8.4. Using VR for Real-Time Feedback

One of the fantastic capabilities of VR is its potential to offer real-time feedback. Various apps and programs provide immediate input on a wide range of performance parameters including voice modulation, use of filler words, eye contact, and body language. This feedback does not merely point at the flaw, but also gives suggestions on how to improve that particular area.

8.5. Practicing Mindfulness with VR

Mindfulness involves focusing one's awareness on the present moment, calmly acknowledging and accepting one's feelings, thoughts, and sensations. This technique is extremely effective in reducing stress and anxiety, enabling you to deliver better speeches. By using relaxation-based VR scenarios prior to the speech practice (a quiet beach or peaceful forest, for instance), you can combine mindfulness practice with exposure therapy for optimum results.

8.6. Reinventing Self-Perception through VR

VR also enables you to view yourself from the audience's perspective. By recording your speech while in VR, you can play it back, experiencing your performance from the other side. It might initially be uncomfortable, but it's an effective tool for understanding your performance and identifying areas of improvement.

8.7. Other VR Features to Consider

Lastly, don't neglect additional benefits that VR can provide. Some advanced VR systems can simulate distractions, heckling, or technology failures, which can be great preparation for real-life unpredictabilities.

Remember that practicing in VR is not a one-time solution. Regular practice is the key. By leveraging the use of this technology, you can surely step forward and transform your public speaking anxieties into charismatic performances. Be sure to embrace the journey and keep in mind that VR is not the magic wand, it's the sword. You are the magician, the warrior who, with time, practice and persistence, will certainly conquer his fears.

VR presents an exciting opportunity — the chance to rehearse and improve away from the glaring spotlight, right in the comfort and privacy of your own space. So, buckle up, put on that VR headset, and step into a world of simulation that feels real. Who knows, you might just find the courage within.

25

Chapter 9. Case Studies of Successful VR Public Speaking Training

Before we delve into the detailed case studies of successful VR Public Speaking Training, let's establish an understanding of what a typical public speaking training session looks like using Virtual Reality. Virtual Reality (VR) utilizes computer technology to place users in an entirely immersive and interactive environment. The applications of VR in public speaking training are vast and impactful. From creating an auditory representation of a large audience to mimicking the intimidating ambiance of speaking at a podium, VR has revolutionized the way public speaking is taught.

9.1. Use Case Study 1: Samsung Gear VR Public Speaking Simulator

One of the most prevalent VR systems used for public speaking training is the Samsung Gear VR Public Speaking Simulator. This system was designed to emulate real life scenarios, from speaking in a small conference room to presenting in a theater filled with hundreds of people.

In this case, a university student named Mark found himself struggling during a public speaking course. His professor noticed his discomfort and suggested he try the Samsung Gear VR Public Speaking Simulator.

Over the course of a few weeks, Mark used the simulator as a supplement to his traditional studies. He was able to practice his speeches in various settings, at different times and under assorted levels of stress. The simulator provided him with an audience that reacted based on his performance which helped him learn to handle anxiety and disruptions.

His progress was evaluated by conducting two assessments; one before commencing the training and the other after completion. The results were striking – Mark's performance improved significantly, his anxiety dropped, and his delivery skills improved drastically.

9.2. Use Case Study 2: VirtualSpeech

Similarly, businesses also attained success using VR public speaking training. A small London-based advertising agency used VirtualSpeech, a VR app that offers public speaking and job interview training.

Faced with a client roster that was constantly expanding, the CEO of the agency realized his employees needed to improve their presentation skills to maintain their quality of service. With the VirtualSpeech app, his employees could experience a range of environments to practice their speeches, receive immediate feedback, and work on areas of improvement.

The results were exceedingly positive. The agency noted an improvement in the clarity and confidence of their employees' presentations. Their pitches became more persuasive, contributing to an enhanced client acquisition rate.

9.3. Use Case Study 3: Sphere

Another instance of successful VR training is the usage of Sphere, a start-up that offers VR-based communication training. This tool was adopted by a political candidate, Lisa, who was preparing for a rigorous election campaign.

Sphere offered Lisa with a whole gamut of scenarios mimicking the high stakes environment of press conferences, town hall meetings, and live interviews. The interactive audience feature, that responded according to Lisa's tone, body language and message content, was instrumental in providing a learning curve that traditional rehearsal methods couldn't deliver.

After weeks of training, Lisa's fear of public speaking was noticeably reduced. Her message delivery became more relaxed and engaging. Ultimately, many believe that her improved public speaking skills, honed via Sphere's VR training, played a significant role in winning her the election.

9.4. Use Case Study 4: Ovation

Last, but not least, is the use of Ovation, a VR service focused on addressing specific fears associated with public speaking such as stage fright, camera shyness, or handling critical questions. A renowned TEDx speaker, preparing for another remarkable address, decided to use Ovation to enhance his performance.

Thanks to the realistic environments and thorough feedback, the speaker noticed a definite decrease in his anxiety levels and an increase in confidence. His TEDx speech was hailed as impressive throughout his industry, showcasing how effectively VR can upgrade the skills of even seasoned public speakers.

In each of these case studies, we see how VR has been used to transform the fear of public speaking into self-assured presentations. From anxious students to seasoned professionals, VR public speaking training has shown definitive success in the growth of its users' abilities. Anyone aiming to improve their performance on the stage should consider such training. VR has truly updated the stage for public speaking training, making it more accessible, adaptable, and comprehensive.

Chapter 10. Creating Effective VR Public Speaking Training Programs

VR technology has radically transformed our capability to tackle public speaking, a skill often seen as daunting by many. By efficiently emulating real-life speaking experiences, it provides a safe, controlled, and highly customizable environment for individuals to practice and enhance their public speaking skills. This safe space allows you to test out speeches, receive feedback, and reduce anxiety - all in a controlled, pressure-free environment. This chapter will provide a comprehensive guide to creating effective VR public speaking training programs.

10.1. Identifying the Audience

Each speaker has a unique audience, which implies that each VR public speaking session should be individually tailored. If you are preparing for a business conference, the VR environment should replicate a professional setting, whereas if you're prepping for a wedding speech, a more informal context should be created. Recognize your audience's demographics, attitudes, and expectations, and incorporate those elements into your VR program for more effective training.

10.2. Developing Realistic Scenarios

An essential aspect to consider when crafting a VR public speaking program is to design as many scenarios as possible to cover all possible occurences. This can range from a small group meeting to a large auditorium filled with hundreds of individuals. Use VR to simulate disturbances such as sudden noises or technical glitches to prepare the speaker for unforeseen circumstances.

10.3. Incorporating Immediate Feedback

The cornerstone of any training is feedback. In a VR public speaking program, immediate feedback on various aspects such as body language, use of filler words, tone of voice, and pacing can be highly beneficial. Record and playback features can be employed to analyze the speaker's performance, followed by helpful suggestions for improvements. This immediate and tailored feedback can lead to quicker improvements in the speaker's abilities.

10.4. Using Biofeedback for Anxiety Management

VR can be coupled with biofeedback devices to track different physiological parameters, such as heart rate, blood pressure, and body temperature, which often increase when a person experiences anxiety. By observing these parameters, speakers can learn to manage their stress responses, and over time, train their bodies to remain calm.

10.5. Gradual Exposure and Practice

Start with smaller, more manageable scenarios to help the user acclimate to VR experiences. Perhaps, first expose users to a small, friendly audience, then gradually increase the size and complexity of the scenarios. The repetitive practice made possible by VR training can significantly help in curbing public speaking anxieties.

10.6. Ensuring Realism through Immersion and Interactivity

Highly detailed graphics, spatialized audio, and responsive virtual audiences contribute to the immersion and interactivity of VR public speaking programs, making them more effective. Higher levels of immersion can help the speaker in better adapting to real-life scenarios.

10.7. Content Preparation in VR

A significant part of public speaking is preparation, and VR can offer an innovative way to help with it. VR environments can help practice delivery of content and provide tools for better preparation like teleprompters or visual aids, thereby helping the speaker be more prepared and confident.

10.8. Performance Analysis and Metrics

VR public speaking programs can provide metrics like speech pace, volume, and pitch modulation to analyze the speaker's performance objectively. These metrics can help the user understand where they are doing well and the areas they need further practice in.

10.9. Continuous Improvement and Updates

Like any training program, a VR public speaking program also needs constant improvement and updates based on the feedback of users and advancements in VR technology. Continuous updates will ensure the program's ongoing relevance and effectiveness.

In conclusion, creating an effective VR public speaking program is about much more than simply replicating a speaking scenario: it's a comprehensive approach that includes understanding the audience, creating realistic environments, offering timely feedback, and incorporating elements of interactivity and immersion. This unique approach will fortify your public speaking skills, and help you feel comfortable and confident every time you take the podium in the real world.

Chapter 11. Potential Pitfalls and How to Overcome Them

Virtual Reality (VR) training for public speaking is a transformative tool, enabling users to overcome personal barriers and improve their presentation skills. However, just like any other tool or methodology, there are potential pitfalls that may hinder your progress. Identifying and understanding these issues will give you a head start in circumventing them, ultimately maximizing your experience and benefits from VR training for public speaking.

11.1. The VR Sickness

One common pitfall encountered by many first-time users of VR is "VR sickness", which includes symptoms such as nausea, headache, or dizziness. It is akin to motion sickness and is caused due to a mismatch between what your eyes see and what your body feels.

One popular method to combat VR sickness is the pause-and-resume strategy. If you start to feel ill during your VR session, immediately remove the headset and take a break. Simple actions like taking deep breaths, drinking water, or having a snack can also help alleviate symptoms.

As you continue with your VR sessions, you may gradually acclimatize to the VR environment and find yourself experiencing fewer and less severe symptoms. However, make sure not to push yourself too hard. If symptoms persist, it would be best to consult with a healthcare professional.

11.2. Dependency on Virtual Reality

While VR is a phenomenal tool for practicing public speaking, it is essential to ensure that it doesn't become a crutch. Remember, the ultimate goal of VR training is not to become an expert speaker in a virtual landscape, but in the real world.

To avoid this pitfall, ensure you balance your practice sessions between the VR platform and real-world opportunities. Look for small forums such as book clubs, community gatherings, or even in front of friends and family where you can apply the skills you've honed in the VR world.

11.3. Overcoming Technical Challenges

VR technology is indeed a complex piece of machinery. Its successful operation requires a suitable device, compatible software, and sometimes even an adequate physical space. Hence, technical glitches can sometimes get in the way of a seamless public speaking training session.

It's important to familiarize yourself with your device and software of choice. Learn how to troubleshoot common problems, like connection issues or hardware compatibility. Also, having a support service contact for your VR provider could come in handy when you face technical challenges beyond your ability.

11.4. Sidestepping Unrealistic Standards

When you see virtual audiences react positively in every scenario in your VR sessions, there's a risk of developing unrealistic standards for real-life experiences. Remember, virtual audiences are designed to mimic real human responses but aren't entirely accurate in every instance.

Understanding that real audiences might not always act as the programmed VR audiences aids in handling real-world situations better. Thus, it's vital to keep expectations realistic when transitioning from VR training to real-life presentations.

11.5. The Data Privacy Concern

Like any other digital technology, VR platforms gather user data. In most cases, this data is used to enhance user experience. However, mishandling of such data can lead to privacy issues.

Ensure that you carefully read through the terms and conditions laid out by your VR service provider. If something seems unclear, don't hesitate to reach out to the provider for clarification. Researching and choosing a reputable VR vendor is crucial in reigning in data privacy concerns.

11.6. Final Thoughts

Virtual Reality offers a promising solution to overcome public speaking fears by providing a safe, controlled, and realistic environment for practice. However, like any tool, it is essential to be aware of its potential pitfalls. By learning to navigate these challenges, you can best harness the power of VR for mastering your public speaking skills.

Remember, each individual's journey with VR will be unique. Success lies not in avoiding obstacles but in learning how to overcome them and adapting along the way. Don't let these challenges deter you. Harness the power of VR and prepare to transform your public speaking skills at your own pace, on your own terms.

Chapter 12. Embracing the Future: A Powerful Speaker Within You

Understanding that fear often acts as an inhibitor to our potential, embracing the future primarily means acknowledging that a powerful speaker already exists within you. It takes an indomitable spirit to set aside fears and anxieties, to focus on growth, and to harness the potential that lies within. Here, in this in-depth look, we explore how you, equipped with the right tools and bolstered by the fantastic world of virtual reality, can transcend the barriers of fear and anxiety to become an impressive public speaker.

12.1. Unveiling Your Hidden Reality

Public speaking, in its essence, is a performance art. It demands a deep understanding of not just what is being communicated but also how it's being delivered. The artistry involved isn't native to all, but it can certainly be developed with the right guidance and resources. What better way, then, to hone this skill than stepping into the virtually real world?

Virtual reality (VR) technology gives you the chance to 'experience' and practice your public speaking skills in a variety of scenarios. Whether it's an auditorium filled with spectators or a boardroom meeting, VR lets you acclimate your senses to different environments and audiences. The first step, therefore, towards embracing the future powerhouse within you is to understand and use VR to simulate real-world speaking situations.

12.2. Fostering Confidence Through Virtual Reality

An essential aspect of being an impactful public speaker is confidence. Conquering the platform and capturing your audience's attention requires a steadfast belief in yourself and in your message. VR technology has a significant role to play here.

In the safe confines of your VR setting, practice different speeches, presentations, or impromptu speaking scenarios. By immersing yourself in VR, you gain the opportunity to confront your fears without the immediate stress of a physical audience. This consistent exposure not only helps you build confidence but also lets you work on your delivery style and body language. Like athletes training their muscles for specific tasks, you are training your mind to be comfortable in the public speaking space.

12.3. Utilizing VR for Feedback and Improvement

One of the more overlooked but critically important aspects of embracing the potential speaker within you is feedback and continuous improvement. Virtual reality technology provides instant feedback on your performance. Applications can provide metrics such as pace, tone, and even monitor eye contact.

The ability to record and play back your sessions provides you with a perspective that live presentations don't usually offer—the perspective of the audience. This allows for targeted improvement and refinement of your skills. It answers essential questions like: Are you using too many filler words? Are you maintaining eye contact? Are you fluctuating your tone appropriately to maintain audience engagement? Such analytical tools within VR applications create a self-regulating path towards improvement.

12.4. From Virtual Reality to Actual Reality: Taking The Step

Ultimately, the aim is to transition your new-found confidence and improved skills from virtual reality to actual reality. Just as a pilot trained on a flight simulator would eventually have to fly a real plane, your goal should be to apply your honed abilities to real-life speaking situations.

COVID-19 has increased the prevalence of virtual meetings and presentations, creating plenty of new opportunities for virtual speakers. Take small steps at first. Seek out opportunities to speak at virtual meetings or webinars before transitioning to larger and more 'real' audiences.

12.5. Conclusion: Embrace the Future!

Embracing the future of public speaking demands a platform where fear is not the controller but a motivator for growth. The amalgamation of VR with the art of public speaking allows you to tap into a resource that melds learning, real-time feedback, and self-improvement into one package.

By fostering confidence through virtual reality, utilizing it for feedback and improvement, and taking incremental steps to transition these experiences into real-life situations, you can unveil the powerhouse speaker within you. Your journey from a novice or a seasoned speaker riddled with anxiety to a confident and impactful orator is not far off. As we navigate this digital age, embrace the future and let your voice be heard. After all, your voice matters, and it's time the world listened.